Ink Stone

Ink Stone

Poems by

Debora Greger

©2017 by the Samuel P. Harn Museum of Art

ISBN 978-0-9833085-5-3

Printed by Alta Systems, Inc.

Design and typesetting by Louise OFarrell

Front cover: Tenkasan Toho (Tenkasan Norio), Japanese,
Tattooed Woman (detail), 1920s. Hanging scroll; ink
and mineral colors on silk, 6 ft. ⅜ in. × 19 ⁵⁄₁₆ in.
(183.9 × 49 cm). Museum purchase, funds provided
by the David A. Cofrin Acquisition Endowment.
2016.67. Photo: Randy Batista

Title page/facing contents: Shibata Zeshin, Japanese
(1807–1891), *Miniature Album of Lacquer Paintings.*
Nineteenth century. Album of 12 leaves; lacquer on paper,
4 ¼ × 3 ⅜ in. (10.8 × 8.5 cm). Museum purchase, funds
provided by the David A. Cofrin Fund for Asian Art.
2016.26. Photo: Randy Batista

HARN MUSEUM OF ART
UNIVERSITY OF FLORIDA

UF | UNIVERSITY *of* FLORIDA

It's not like anything
they compare it to—
   the summer moon.

     *

When the winter chrysanthemums go
there's nothing to write about
   but radishes.

     *

As for the hibiscus
on the roadside—
   my horse ate it.

—Basho

Table of Contents

Preface

In 2008, Jason Steuber began working at the Harn Museum of Art as the inaugural Cofrin Curator of Asian Art, an endowed chair. By good fortune and timing, University of Florida Professor Debora Greger began holding poetry class at the Harn that year.

One day in Spring 2009, students and professor gathered around the Chinese scholar rocks in the Axline Asian Art Gallery, talking about how stones inspired writers. Dr. David A. Cofrin happened upon the group and was so impressed he proceeded to demonstrate the beautiful sound his collection of scholars' rock made when thumped by his wedding ring. And so collaborations between Debora and the Harn through poetry and events came into being. In 2010, she was asked to compose a poem for the museum's 20th anniversary publication. Her subject: those rocks. In the same milestone catalogue, she also contributed a poem on the museum's *Champ d'avoine (Oat Field)* by Claude Monet. Her official role as Harn Poet-In-Residence evolved from the mentoring of an undergraduate intern. Anna Mebel, a UF honors student majoring in English and art history, wanted to do a poetry project, of all things, for Opening Day of the Asian Art Wing in March, 2012. Debora was brought on board to lend a guiding hand with Anna's Japanese renga-writing activity for visitors. Person by person, stanza by stanza, a collaborative poem was created. By the end of that afternoon, the two of them were invited to stay on as the museum's first Poets-in-Residence.

Debora has since hosted seven undergraduate and graduate interns of various academic disciplines and experience, from art history through English to creative writing and law. She arrives for her museum meetings with piles of Asian poetry books for each of her interns, often so many they are toted in public library sacks! Anna's internship project created a template for the Museum Nights activity the Poets-in-Residence contribute to. Once a month on a Thursday evening, when the galleries are open late, students and community members watch performances, take tours, attend lectures, make art; once a semester they write about what they've seen. Ask a visitor to write a poem—and many flee. The poets found ingenious ways around the public's seeming fear of poetry: make collaborative lists in the style of medieval Japanese writer Sei Shōnagon, fold origami love knots, build origami memory palaces story by story, compose conversations between art and everyday objects.

Debora's poems for the museum catalog provided another template for what poets could contribute to the museum. One of the most rewarding experiences for the curators has been time spent with the poets down in art storage. Viewings, scheduled several times a semester, feature objects to be installed in coming months up in the galleries. Poets have created pieces vividly describing a single object, contemplated a series of prints in an exhibition, and experimented with various Asian poetry forms. This volume is a compilation of the poems composed by Debora Greger during her tenure as Poet-in-Residence (2010–2017). Recent exhibitions that provided an opportunity for study have included *ClayCurvyCool*, featuring contemporary Japanese ceramics, and *Show Me the Mini*, a pan-Asian art show centered on the diminutive.

We wholeheartedly thank Debora Greger for her dedication to the poets-in-residence program and for her works inspired by the collections. The UF students who joined her in getting this program to soar deserve our thanks too: Anna Mebel, Angela Li, Elaina Mercatoris, Cary Marcous, Eileen Rush, Emily Merritt, and Giavanna Landicini. Our thanks also are due to Rebecca Nagy, Director of the Harn Museum of Art, for her support and enthusiasm for this innovative and collaborative program.

In recognition and celebration of the Harn Poet-In-Residence program's first decade, we are proud to present this volume of poetry and hope that readers will find as much enjoyment in these lines as we have.

Jason M. Steuber, Cofrin Curator of Asian Art
Allysa B. Peyton, Assistant Curator of Asian Art

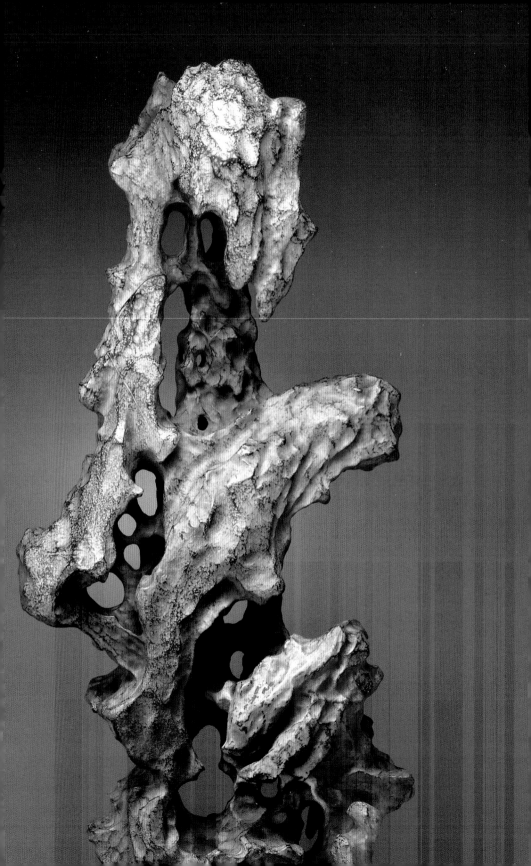

A Scholar's Rock Looks at a Poet

The rock said:
I love the way those old drunks wrote,
all that dew, moon, rain on bamboo, etc.
They wrote on paintings. They wrote on jade
to stop the knife cutting deeper.

They wrote and drank, drank and wrote.
And they always said "I,"
especially when no one was home
at the hut where they stopped
on their way to exile even more remote.

They left a poem to say
life would likely never send them by again
but friend, don't cut that bamboo—
wait till snow gives it a blanket
beautiful enough to take your breath away

from the cold, loneliness, etc.
The drunken Minister on Distant Service
to Celestial Principalities, banished Immortal,
envoy on earth of thirty-six Heavenly Rulers,
Person in Plain Clothes

who leaned from his boat
to scoop the dripping moon into his arms—
or so poets claim: I like him.
He drowned as stone does, cleanly,
leaving no account. After that,

what were a few more centuries?
I am still here. I don't reveal my age.
Where is the wind that played the jade reed-pipe?
Where the wind that never finished
wearing me down to sand?

The Monet Returns from its Travels

Champ d'avoine

Claude Monet

I.

The painting said, In a room of Monets,
I was just another acre of paint,

a field of oats, a summer lost
somewhere in France.

Wild poppies tip their papery cups
to call for light, more light,

another goblet of red, please,
though it's nowhere near noon—

see how last night's dregs
pool under my trees, the blue of distance

edging a blade, an ear,
drawing it near to push it away.

II.

I missed the way in Florida,
before the museum opens,

at the rushy rim of the pond out back,
yellow soup-bowls of American lotus—

your country's largest bloom—
set themselves out as if for *le dejeuner*

in the deep-yellow dining-room
of Monsieur l'artiste in Giverny.

Down Museum Road, mist huffs on the mirror
of Lake Alice until it clears:

a great blue heron wades his reflection.
That feather—burnt sienna or smoke

impossible to mix? Until the next meal
swims up, the bird holds still as a dancer

pirouetted from a Degas. Not so,
the blunt, smug blade of alligator

cutting the glass to *before* and *after*.

Still Life with Dead Letter: Mme Sévigné in New York

French Literature

Bradley Walker Tomlin

I.

Mme. wrote, *Stag-hunting by moonlight.*
Lanterns' brilliance eclipsed the play.
Supper served in a glade carpeted with jonquils—
and not enough roast for the retinue.

Fireworks, at sixteen thousand francs,
failed on account of fog. Next morning,
the fish did not arrive. Fearing dishonor,
the steward absented himself.

In chambers, his sword, stood against the door,
passed on the third stab through his heart.
In a pool of blood, he was found
just as the ordered fish at last appeared.

The royal party dined, they strolled,
they hunted and feasted to the scent of narcissus.
Only at nightfall did the King depart
at last for another palace—

where he could order a midnight meal,
of the quantum devoured after a fast.

II.

Mme. said, Death is not life
       in a French village.
It is the New World of Manahatta,
       which stinks of home:

sweat, perfume, ordure. Sausage
       not worthy of the name
but a heretic laid over coals until charred.
       Brioches tied into knots

like brides on their wedding nights.
       Night? There be none.
And Death? A tower among towers,
       ascended in a closet

rising on ropes, pulled by—but
       one never sees.
About this chair—claimed Louis XIV,
       I have grave doubts.

The demilune under a martello
       of French books?
Veneer crazed, legs not original—
       I recognize

arranged marriage when I behold it.

Vermeer
in Japan

Daydreaming

Suzuki Yasuyuki

No protected world
   —"Vermeer,"
Tomas Tranströmer

Behind the bare wall,
a laugh, a howl, a temple bell—
then something began to gnaw:
the rat beloved of netsuke carvers.

In a desk chair dying to swivel,
shipped from a country she'd seen in a magazine,
where women in the latest fashions
posed like statues afraid to wrinkle,

a woman sat, hair bobbed and crimped
in waves Hiroshige would recognize.
She wore silk hose—but still removed her shoes
at the door. In her lap lay a sketchbook,

an open boat aground on her skirt.
A woman is an island. Beyond the wall,
her archipelago loved a border war.
The emperor wanted Manchuria.

What did *she* want? She gazed
past a scratching in the wall.
A stowaway brought by tall Dutch ships
to a port named Nagasaki,

the brown rat curled on himself,
thing of beauty in the hand
of Death, the great netsuke carver.

Postcards from the Tokaido Road

*The Fifty-Three
Stations of the
Tokaido Road*

Hiroshige

Station 1. *Bridge, Nihon-bashi*

From the fish market at the bridge,
they have started across: two geishas,
kimonos woven of water crossing over sky.

Caught on the silk: the salty musk
of creatures that don't belong on land.
The powdered moons of the women's faces:

paper left raw. In the half-open lily
of her hand, one holds a puppet
as if, tighter, something would break.

Station 16. *Woman Reading, Kambara*

She has pinned back her bangs,
drawn the rest aside with a rag.
She can't put the story down.

The hand that holds the book open
barely emerges from her kimono.
Has a passage trudged a mountain pass?

Twelve volumes from now, the heroine—
sneaking from home by night
to follow the traveler she fell in love with,

then taking his long road north on foot—
will die, a crumple of paper, at this station.
The woman by the window feels a chill:

by snowlight, Fuji reads over her shoulder.

Station 18. *The Poet on Tago Beach*

Draped over beach-pine to dry,
the fish nets fail to stir—
sea breeze picks on the poet instead.

He thought he had the beach to himself.
Now his hat would take flight.
His robe flaps, longing to be a kite.

What does the bay scribble, then erase,
starting over on the way to open water?
To the mountain drawing nearer,

paper has never been more exquisitely empty
than its slopes. *From across the bay,*
the poet wrote a thousand years ago,

I see one whiteness fall upon another—
on Fuji's peak, first snow.

Station 29. *First Shogun and Cranes*

From a mound of blue brocade
settled in billows on the shore,
the sea withdraws, scraping and bowing:

today the first shogun takes the salt air,
along with his foothills. One holds a parasol
over the snow of his ruler's forehead.

The huge wings of a question hover:
how long does the red-crowned crane live?
A thousand years? He commands

the date be tied to the legs of a thousand birds.
Up airy stairs they climb.
How long will *he* live?

All this will not be his much longer,
but what of that? Wavelets march by, aglint,
rank upon rank demanding his review.

Station 32. *Travel Diary*

Dusk. An actor made up to play
Woman with Travel Diary pauses
on the bridge, brush in mouth,

diary blank, to admire the twilight
a prince captured, and better,
six hundred springs before:

Dusk. The washing of the shore goes on.
Drowned sighs of scrubby pines.
The bridge wraps itself in a shroud of mist.

Station 39. *The Tomb of Love*

Moonless. By the light of plum blossom,
the castle gate opens enough for a woman
in a coat of midnight to slip out. But wait!

Checking over her shoulder that no one sees,
a maid holds out the rain hat forgotten.
Where is she going on foot, alone?

Where lovesickness leads.
Does Love match her step on the road north?
Death is the shadow in this land without them,

dogging her, running her down.

Station 40. *The Poet, Eight Bridges*

What is sky but water
crossed by eight bridges?
Does he rush to reach dry land?

No, he's already an Immortal.
How long before the water iris he came to admire,
taking their time to unscroll,

wither to paper? They barely grow beards.
In a thousand years, pilgrims will come
to stand where he stood. Where, they will ask,

are the flowers that empurpled his poem?

Station 44. *Mirage of Summer*

Pennons salute a breeze unbent,
bent back on itself, but she eyes the bank,
we can't see. Where in summer

a mirage appeared: the Clam's Palace,
also called Going-to-visit-the-god-at-his-shrine.
She's going nowhere. Chin on one hand,

she gazes as if today no mirage will fade,
tomorrow no season begin to end.

To an Inkstone

You lost footprint, fill!
    Little mudhole gone dry—
oh, for an ounce of water to brim your hollow.
    Where's your inkstick of soot and glue?
In relief, a dragon gnaws a flaming pearl.
    Stone, I want a drink.

Celadon bowl, I apologize.
    I thought you were empty—

but you with your secrets,
    all gray-green:

you're the prairie's great sinkhole.
    An alligator opens a seam across silk.

The Dead

Akoda Pumpkin

Katsumata Chieko

I. The Dead of Night

The clay pumpkin said,
In the museum of moonlight, I look real,
though I lack a slug bite.

I lack the petitions of a snail Marco Polo.
Liar, traveler, nightly he would drag the palazzo
of lies along the Silk road of a garden.

Would he chance a shortcut
up the perilous ascent of a pumpkin,
silvering the route with slime?

Earthiest of odalisques, in my vitrine
I repose on the memory of dirt.
A rat skitters past a netsuke of rats.

A flashlight walks its guard.

II. The Dead of Summer

All summer it hid under its leaves,
out of sight of the sun. It hid from us.
Fallout we couldn't see found it.

Radiation monitor by day, evening gardener,
Father knew where the pumpkin lolled.
In a palace of jade shadow, it fattened.

Child astrologers, we searched dark skies
for Sputnik-1 or -2. For the dog cosmonaut
trapped in one of them, did we pray?

Mornings pressed us to servitude.
First Brother slopped the scalded fruit
in front of Second Sister, who slipped the skins.

Mother taped her thumb lest she cut herself,
then sliced lopsided globs in two.
Eldest but with the slimmest hand,

I fed them, finger by finger, to narrow-mouth jars.
Glassed in, sealed, too beautiful to eat,
the dead of summer awaited the dead of winter.

Fold upon Fold

pli selon pli
—Stephane Mallarmé

Pli Selon Pli

Akiyama Yō

I. Across the Country

my dead mother flew.
Had she been to this museum?
She had no sense of direction.

At yards of clay unfolded on the floor
she said, "Didn't I leave you
Vice President of Folding the Laundry?

You didn't fold my ashes.
You didn't fold up the river
after your father spilled my urn in it."

A swan bore a bead of water
on its back across the river of forgetting.
Where did I leave my suitcase,

the one that held everything I forgot?
Packing took forever, fold upon fold
upon fold. Which daughter was I?

She folded them all together.

II. At Length

down the two-lane road from childhood,
we came to a sign so deep in nowhere,
it said DO NOT STOP. DO NOT TAKE PHOTOGRAPHS.

There was nothing to shoot
but a tumbleweed on the run.
Wind pushed rabbitbrush aside.

Who pressed the ribbon of river?
A darning needle of smokestack
wavered above the eggshell of reactor dome.

Farther away, in a war always cold,
an iron curtain rusted shut.
But across the river, time lay down,

fold upon igneous, exhausted fold.
Basalt opened fists into fat-fingered hills.
Motherly, the lithic pressure.

Skin of Clay

Akiyama Yō, School
of Art & Art History

He let clay do his talking.
To the mud, he spoke with his hands,
        but first

he listened to it. Out the window,
the sun waxed a wave of traffic stalled
        in Florida.

On a folding chair, I folded myself
under a lazy snow of clay dust—
        why was I

in black? I couldn't change:
I had entered a room in Kyoto.
        The man

slapped clay into a minor moon.
He'd peel it like a tangerine,
        the translator said.

But first he had to give it a skin—
he lit a blowtorch, though he wore no gloves.
        "Why do you strip me

from myself?" Marsyas howled. For daring
to challenge the flute of a god.
        The skin lay open.

Lungs filled but not with air.
A heart flooded, chamber by chamber.

Ink Garden

I. Wet

To soar is to fall,
the hawk said to the lamp post
where it perched.

You stop rowing the wings,
trusting the heat
to open its hand beneath you—

but you're distracted
by a gash in the sky below: a lizard
treading the air

from stalk to stone. In the water garden
(blue postage stamp
licked to a postcard of lawn)

the anolis rules.
He puffs the blood petal at his throat.
He was a butterfly,

he dreamed—or did the eyespots
of dusty wings
see themselves as a chameleon's?

Outgrowing a skin,
he devours it. To escape the talons
of Death,

he shed his tail. Another grew,
less whippy,
but *l'empereur-philosophe* still reigns.

Dare a mosquito
charge across the footbridge,
straight pin drawn?

II. Dry

The gravel said,
When were we next door
    to the Atlas Mountains?
Continents drifted apart like families.

They broke us up
for railroad ballast, then shunted
    that golden age
down a siding to rust. They sold us off,

crushed to peas
for landscapers. Sifted, graded,
    the mountain came
to the museum of leftovers.

On the roof
of the loading dock, they laid
    a dry garden.
The gardener asked its standing stones

what they needed.
To be islands! He had an ocean
    of gravel to rake.
Does he ask what's underfoot?

We weren't always
Salt and Pepper Aggregate Size 3.
    We're watered, combed
into rollers, crisp as new money

The world is empty,
lord, empty of a self, of anything
    close to a self.

The Alley Behind Memory

Box Orange-05T

Kimiyo Mishima

I.

Down a blind alley, the rain swept,
     a drop ahead of me.
          On a wounded chair

behind a store, a box slumped.
     Once it bore an orange on wings
        over an ocean.

It carried the legend still,
     characters swishing like mandarins.
        A crumple of old news

cushioned a teapot that brooded,
     marooned as a hen.
        China lifted its beak
            to drink the rain red glaze preening.

II.

I knew the alley. I dream-walked the town.
In my father's garden,
red ran down

my arm from the first bite of summer.
It splattered my first glasses.
O tomato,

cultured by horse manure and Haydn!
Where sprinklers reigned at dawn,
Father and his tubers

listened to radio till it was time for him
to disappear into the desert
toward the reactor.

At dusk, child war whoops braided
with chamber music.
I swallowed

a slurp of hose water: it tasted
unearthed, worm-wandered,
sunburnt.

III.

Decades would be cast on his compost pile
before Father at ninety,
planting a garden—

a tub by the back door, a few
Early Girl tomatoes—
would be interrupted

by a visitor he hadn't seen since the winter
never mentioned, the one
on the Maginot Line.

Seventy years ago in the Ardennes,
Death had come for the man
next to him instead.

The Elephant
God Speaks

Ganesha

Those cakes you leave me,
golden figs, encrusted moons—I like them.

To taste the way an elephant scratched
against a tree that a boy climbed barefoot,

bearing a fierce knife—I accept that as my due.
Back they wander, boy and beast,

with a nut the size of a human head—
I was never an elephant with a broken tusk.

Was I ever a boy? I've been a god too long.
I, Lord of Obstacles—do I place them

in your path, or push them away?
Lord of Letters, I chew over yours,

then have to spit. Lord of New Beginnings,
I proclaim, Let there be cakes, more cakes!

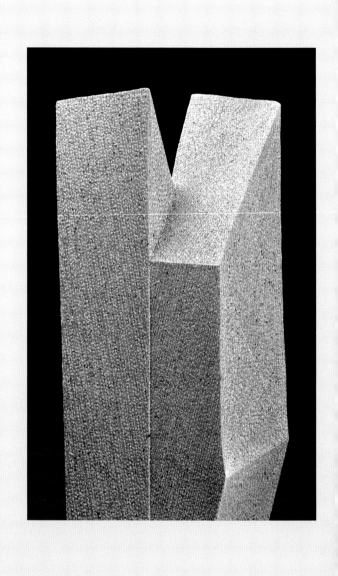

Small Monument in Memory of Winter

Untitled

Kishi Eiko

Under a cold blanket, yellow blades slept,
the lullaby of the lawn all scrunches and squeaks
as cars furrowed and fishtailed the street.
From our roof, an icicle forest grew,
worth saving for the county fair—worth
laying beside carrots competing for ribbons.
Wadded in woolens, stiff as a snowman,
I studied a sky stuffing more secrets into clouds.
Father sniffed the air, a boy on a farm again,
catching the drift of snow driven to bury the Plains.
I knew nothing. But we had winters then.

Against
Moonlight

Moonlight

Fukumoto Fuku

Selfish the moon, silken and solitary. If a guard,
by night, drops a tear into your bowl, if Mare
Crisium overflows, how many other craters lie
coldly, gathering dust? Sea of Clouds, Lake
of Dreams, Ocean of Storms: how much
do the names we pinned to you weigh?
Because you make demands, moon.
Now you want to be carried—you,
the child who claims it's too far
from one night to the next.

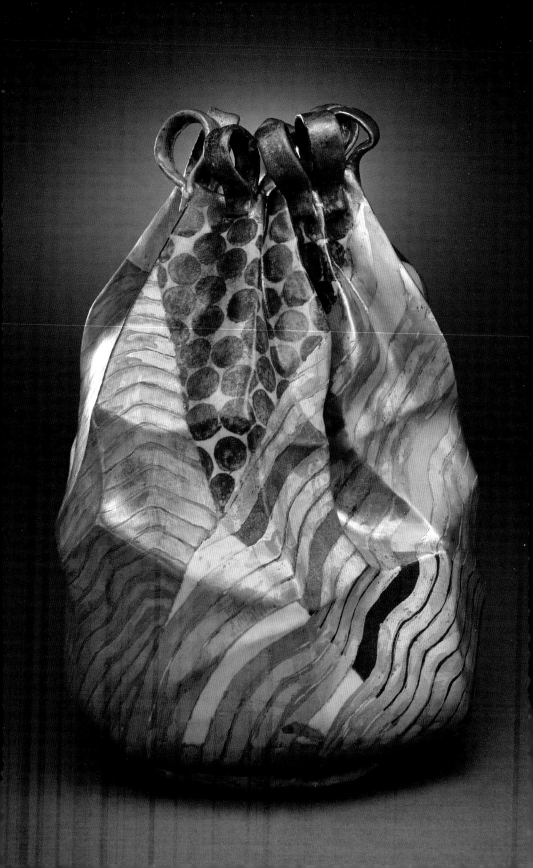

Never Closer

Refined Silk

Tsuboi Asuka

O, O, O, O, O,
Venice, sunk in reflection!
Across a footbridge
lay Marco Polo's house.
At a long window, his ghost
studied a scribble of sunlight
on the canal. The jewels he secreted
in his Tartar coat for the journey home—
gone. Traded away, his miles of China silk
for furs and food, potions he had to trust
would cure, not kill. Endless that ocean
of sand, its noons eternal. Ghost palazzi
shimmered on ghost lagoons,
never drawing near.

On a Scholar's Desk

Scholar's rock

I. Handful of Scholar's Rock

The rock said, I was a mountain once.
    I wore a glacier like a mink.
        Now I fit

the hand that wouldn't leave me
    where I came to rest.
        He stood me

on his desk; I longed to lie down.
    Did he write out the clouds
        he claimed

I suggested—fog on a peak, white cry
    of a crane flying north
        unseen, etc.?

Down I tumbled, scroll after scroll.
    I remember a clatter,
        river by stream.

Each body of water sanded my skin.

II. Out of Paper

A breeze
muscled into the room.
It dragged a brush across a page—

the scholar
reached for a paperweight,
hand falling on a wasp nest.

Of ebony.
Some cells stayed empty
some cradled larvae of deer antler, awaiting

their next life.

Wasp nest *okimono*

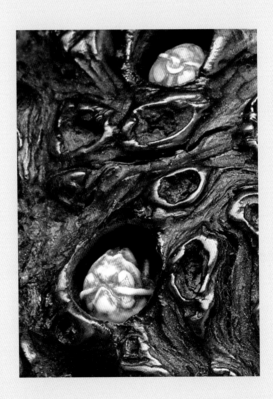

III. Drawdown

Not Sunday,
mud-day! Drawdown
at a dam upstream lay bare a past—

the ancient
flood plain of a river
I thought I knew. Into life surprised

to death,
we squelched, my father and I.
That packed circle of earth? Site of a tipi.

Waterweed
dried into parchment
too late for treaties. Stranded salmon,

wind socks
in death, eyed river-licked granite
until it blushed. The brass button of a beetle

got a last spit
and polish. Notched twice
where knapped—in the sea of pebbles,

Father found
a net-sinker, then another—
how, when I had sloshed right over them?

Untitled T-026

Akiyama Yō

Bunchin (paperweight)

Okada Yūji

Miniature album of
lacquer paintings

Shibata Zeshin

IV. Forever the Approach

Forever, the approach down a valley of dirt
between carrots and lettuce!
How long, ant,

had you been climbing a cucumber
on the vine? Long ago,
this morning,

I was ten, a tomato ripe enough to burst
in one hand, your cucumber
in the other.

Ant, I apologize. You escaped my notice
till you tumbled to the mud.
Shadows deepen

we'll have to bridge—by the time
we reach evening,
I'll be over sixty.

Forked under for good, this garden by then.
Its gardener, my father,
turned to ash.

Cabinet
of Wonder

Clam shell-form
box

I. Inside a Shell

i. Silver Clam

One morning
in the Tang, someone opened
this silver clam and began seven stages

of painting her face.
To show she didn't work the fields,
she scooped crushed mother-of-pearl.

Gold she sealed
to her brow with a roll of jade.
Dimples needed paint. Too flat, her cheeks.

Vermilion redrew
the lips. New eyebrows peaked
like Mount Fuji. Of the finished face

she gazed upon?
The silver clam lay, shut,
beached on silk behind glass.

ii. Butter Clam

From its fat book, the Pacific ripped
        another page, too big
            to turn.

It lunged at my bare feet but I dug on—
        down to China, it seemed,
            yet the clam

dug faster. Or my arm grew shorter.
        Wet sand took my shape.
            I was flotsam,

the tide tossing the next page of salt
        over my calves. Up squalled a gull,
            empty-beaked.

II. After the Afterlife

We drifted, my dead parents and I,
    past the jade, the celadon.
        At the grave goods,

they stopped and would not be moved.
    How small they'd grown.
        Like children,

they climbed the model Ming chairs
    to see a feast of clay
        spread for them.

With finger bone, Father touched the head
    of a boar on a platter.
        Lost pig pen

of youth! After supper, the youngest son
    hauled the scraps pigward,
        then leaned

Tomb models
of domestic
furnishings

on the fence in the squeals and grunts.
    Death leaned beside him.

Peach cup

III. Under the Underworld

Back to their dark beneath the stairs,
    canning jars straggled, empty
        of summer.

Gone, peach jam infused with August,
    relish tinged with frost.
        Gone,

the orchard we picked our way through,
    fruit dusted with DDT.
        That land

lies in a lattice crust of streets
    named for the uprooted,
        the burned.

Mother preserved everything but herself.
    Her ashes fit in a jar.
        A skin

I slipped from a blanched peach
    decades ago hardened
        into this cup

from the Qing, cinnabar on ivory,
    silver-lined as if
        with lead.

IV. Found Empty

i.

> To enter,
> I had to leave belongings
> at the door. One gallery after another
> didn't bother to rouse
> for a visitor
>
> alone
> Painted to feathered
> stillness, a great blue heron knew,
> like Father, a master
> didn't pursue;
>
> he let the fish
> come to him. Where it fell
> to a shelf, a leaf gone white readied
> to ferry an insect
> in flood waters.

Forest with Heron

Herman Herzog

Leaf-shaped dish

Mushikago
(*Cricket Cage*)

Nozaki Sadao

ii.

In the last room
I found two young women—
nearly my sister and myself, years ago.

But on the scroll,
the elder wore kimono,
the younger had bobbed hair.

What wrinkled
her slim ankles? Fashion
from the West: her first silk stockings.

In a cage,
the sisters kept a cricket
for its song. The paper-lantern flush,

the inking
of a summer evening,
the veranda of Japan, 1930—

O lost wings!
Your brittle exoskeleton
the soft underparts devoured long ago.

Illustrations

China

Upright Scholar's Rock
Nineteenth–twentieth
century
Lingbi stone, wood base
45 x 20 x 14 in.
(114.3 x 50.8 x 35.6 cm)
Museum purchase,
funds provided by
friends of the Harn
Museum
2006.21.4
Photo: Randy Batista
Poem: page 1

Claude Monet, French
(1840–1926)

*Champ d'avoine
(Oat Field)*
1890
Oil on canvas
26 x 36 ⁷⁄₁₆ in.
(66 x 92.6 cm)
Gift of Michael A. Singer
1999.6
Photo: Randy Batista
Poem: page 2

Bradley Walker Tomlin,
American (1899–1953)

French Literature

c. 1930

Oil on canvas

20 1/16 x 24 1/8 in.
(51 x 61.3 cm)

Gift of Caroline Julier
Richardson

1991.20.2

Photo: Randy Batista

Poem: page 4

Suzuki Yasuyuki,
Japanese (1911–1980)

Daydreaming

1938–1940

Painting on paper in
mineral pigments and
sumi ink

Inclusive of frame:
5 ft. 2 1/4 in. x 46 1/4 in.
(158.1 x 117.5 cm)

Museum purchase,
funds provided by the
Caroline Julier and
James G. Richardson
Acquisition Funds
and the Gladys Harn
Harris Art Acquisition
Endowment

2013.59.1

Poem: page 6

Utagawa Kuniyoshi
(1798–1861)

Nihonbashi, from the
series *Tōkaidō gojūsan
tsugi*
Edo Period (1615–
1867), 1845
Color woodcut; ink and
color on paper
14 ⅜ x 9 ¾ in.
(36.5 x 24.8 cm)
Museum purchase,
gift of friends of the
museum
2005.25.7.1
Photo: Randy Batista
Poem: page 8

Utagawa Kuniyoshi
(1798–1861)

Kambara, from the
series *Tōkaidō gojūsan
tsugi*
Edo Period (1615–
1867), 1845
Color woodcut; ink and
color on paper
14 ⅜ x 9 ¾ in.
(36.5 x 24.8 cm)
Museum purchase,
gift of friends of the
museum
2005.25.7.16
Photo: Randy Batista
Poem: page 9

Utagawa Hiroshige
(1797–1858)

Okitsu, from the series
Tōkaidō gojūsan tsugi
Edo Period (1615–
1867), 1845
Color woodcut; ink and
color on paper
14 ⅜ x 9 ¾ in.
(36.5 x 24.8 cm)
Museum purchase,
gift of friends of the
museum
2005.25.7.18
Photo: Randy Batista
Poem: page 10

Utagawa Kuniyoshi
(1798–1861)

Mitsuke, from the
series *Tōkaidō gojūsan
tsugi*
Edo Period (1615–
1867), 1845
Color woodcut; ink and
color on paper
14 ⅜ x 9 ¾ in.
(36.5 x 24.8 cm)
Museum purchase,
gift of friends of the
museum
2005.25.7.29
Photo: Randy Batista
Poem: page 11

Utagawa Kunisada
(1786–1865)

Arai, from the series
Tōkaidō gojūsan tsugi
Edo Period (1615–
1867), 1845
Color woodcut; ink and
color on paper
14 ³⁄₈ x 9 ³⁄₄ in.
(36.5 x 24.8 cm)
Museum purchase,
gift of friends of the
museum
2005.25.7.32
Photo: Randy Batista
Poem: page 12

Utagawa Hiroshige
(1797–1858)

Okazaki, from the
series *Tōkaidō gojūsan
tsugi*
Edo Period (1615–
1867), 1845
Color woodcut; ink and
color on paper
14 ³⁄₈ x 9 ³⁄₄ in.
(36.5 x 24.8 cm)
Museum purchase,
gift of friends of the
museum
2005.25.7.39
Photo: Randy Batista
Poem: page 13

Utagawa Kuniyoshi
(1798–1861)

Chiryū, from the series
Tōkaidō gojūsan tsugi

Edo Period (1615–
1867), 1845

Color woodcut; ink and
color on paper

14 ³⁄₈ x 9 ¾ in.
(36.5 x 24.8 cm)

Museum purchase,
gift of friends of the
museum

2005.25.7.40

Photo: Randy Batista

Poem: page 14

Utagawa Kunisada
(1786–1865)

Yokkaichi, from the
series *Tōkaidō gojūsan
tsugi*

Edo Period (1615–
1867), 1845

Color woodcut; ink and
color on paper

14 ³⁄₈ x 9 ¾ in.
(36.5 x 24.8 cm)

Museum purchase,
gift of friends of the
museum

2005.25.7.44

Photo: Randy Batista

Poem: page 15

Korea

Inkstone
Joseon dynasty (1392–
1910), late nineteenth
century
Stone
2 ³/₈ x 10 ⅛ x 7 ⅝ in.
(6 x 25.7 x 19.4 cm)
In Memory of John
Wilson Reynolds, Jr.
2008.35
Photo: Randy Batista
Poem: page 16

Korea

*Celadon Dish with
Impressed Floral Design*
Goryeo dynasty (918–
1392), twelfth–thirteenth
century
Glazed stoneware
1 ⅞ x 6 ⅝ x 6 ⅝ in.
(4.8 x 16.8 x 16.8 cm)
Gift of General James A.
Van Fleet
1988.1.15
Photo: Randy Batista
Poem: page 17

Katsumata Chieko,
Japanese (b. 1950)

Akoda Pumpkin

2013

Stoneware

15 ¾ x 17 ⁵⁄₁₆ x 15 ⅜ in.
(40 x 44 x 39 cm)

Loan of Carol and
Jeffrey Horvitz

Photo: Randy Batista

Poem: page 18

Akiyama Yō, Japanese (b. 1953)

Pli Selon Pli

2002

Stoneware

26 ¾ in. x 11 ft. 5 ¾ in. x 47 ¼ in.
(67.9 x 349.9 x 120 cm)

Collection of Carol and Jeffrey Horvitz

Installation view at the Harn Museum of Art, 2014

Photo: Randy Batista

Poem: page 20

Akiyama Yō
Demonstration at
University of Florida
College of the Arts
November 3, 2014
Photo: Ray Carson
Poem: page 23

Waterfall
Water Garden, David A.
Cofrin Asian Art Wing
Photo: Austin Bell
Poem: page 24

Rock Garden, David A.
Cofrin Asian Art Wing
Photo: Randy Batista
Poem: page 25

Kimiyo Mishima, Japanese
(b. 1932)

Box Orange—05T

2005

Glazed stoneware,
newspaper, teapot

11 ½ x 12 ¾ x 10 in.
(29.2 x 32.4 x 25.4 cm)

Museum purchase, gift
of the Jeffrey E. Horvitz
Foundation in honor of
Budd Harris Bishop

2008.25.4

Photo: Randy Batista
Poem: page 26

India, Bengal

Ganesha

Seventeenth century

Bronze

Height: 2 ⅜ in. (6 cm)

Gift of George P. Bickford

S-69-36

Photo: Randy Batista

Poem: page 29

Kishi Eiko, Japanese (b. 1948)

Untitled (Sculptural Form)

2007

Stoneware with inlay

32 ½ x 11 ¾ x 6 ¼ in. (82.6 x 29.8 x 15.9 cm)

Museum purchase, gift of the Jeffrey E. Horvitz Foundation in honor of Budd Harris Bishop

2008.25.3

Photo: Randy Batista

Poem: page 31

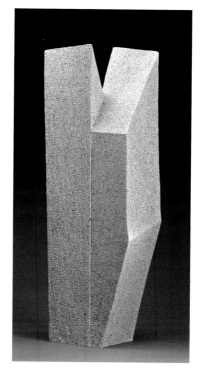

Fukumoto Fuku, Japanese
(b. 1973)

Moonlight (Tsuki kage)

2009

Porcelain

9 ¼ x 15 ¼ x 15 ½ in.
(23.5 x 38.7 x 39.4 cm)

Gift of Carol and Jeffrey
Horvitz

2016.76.4

Photo: Randy Batista

Poem: page 32

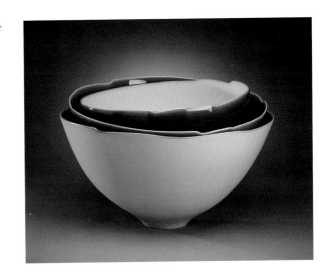

Tsuboi Asuka, Japanese
(b. 1932)

*Refined Silk, Kyoto Wave
("Neriginu: Kyo No
Nami")*

2015

Stoneware

9 ¹⁄₁₆ × 6 ⅞ × 6 ¹¹⁄₁₆ in.
(23 × 17.5 × 17 cm)

Loan from the collection
of Carol and Jeffrey
Horvitz

Photo: Randy Batista

Poem: page 35

China

Scholar's Rock
Qing dynasty (1644–1911)
Jade, wood
3 x 2 ¹⁄₁₆ x 1 ⁹⁄₁₆ in.
(7.6 x 5.2 x 4 cm)
Bequest of Dr. David A.
Cofrin
2009.48.83
Photo: Randy Batista
Poem: page 36

Japan

Wasp Nest Okimono
Late Meiji Period, c.
1890–1912
Ebony, stag antler
2 × 3 ½ × 2 ⅞ in.
(5.1 × 8.9 × 7.3 cm)
Museum purchase, funds
provided by the Kathleen
M. Axline Acquisition
Endowment
2016.59.2
Photo: Randy Batista
Poem: page 37

Akiyama Yō, Japanese
(b. 1953)

Untitled T-026

2002

Unglazed stoneware

10 ¼ x 23 ¼ x 14 ⁹⁄₁₆ in.
(26 x 59 x 37 cm)

Museum purchase,
funds provided by The
David A. Cofrin Fund
for Asian Art

2014.37

Photo: Randy Batista

Poem: page 38

Okada Yūji, Japanese
(b. 1948)

Bunchin (*Paperweight*)

2016

Stone, gold, silver,
lacquer, mother-of-pearl

1 ¼ × 3 ⅛ × 2 ⅛ in.
(3.2 × 7.9 × 5.4 cm)

Museum purchase, funds
provided by the Kathleen
M. Axline Acquisition
Endowment

2016.59.3

Photo: Randy Batista

Poem: page 38

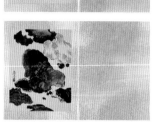

Shibata Zeshin, Japanese
(1807–1891)

*Miniature Album of
Lacquer Paintings*
Nineteenth century
Album of 12 leaves;
lacquer on paper

4 ¼ × 3 ⅜ in. (10.8 × 8.5 cm)

Museum purchase, funds provided
by the David A. Cofrin Fund for
Asian Art

2016.26

Photo: Randy Batista

Poem: page 39

China

Clam Shell-Form Box
Tang dynasty (618–907)
Silver
⅞ x 1 ½ x 1 ⁵⁄₁₆ in.
(2.2 x 3.8 x 3.3 cm)
Bequest of Dr. David A.
Cofrin
2009.48.71
Photo: Randy Batista
Poem: page 40

China

Tomb Models of Domestic Furnishings
Ming dynasty (1368–1644), fifteenth–sixteenth century
Glazed earthenware
Dimensions variable
Museum purchase, gift of Ruth Pruitt Phillips
2000.6
Photo: Randy Batista
Poem: page 42

China

Peach Cup
Qing dynasty (1644–1911)
Ivory, silver, and cinnabar
lacquer
$^{15}/_{16}$ x 2 ½ x 1 ¾ in.
(2.4 x 6.4 x 4.4 cm)
Bequest of Dr. David A.
Cofrin
2009.48.64
Photo: Randy Batista
Poem: page 43

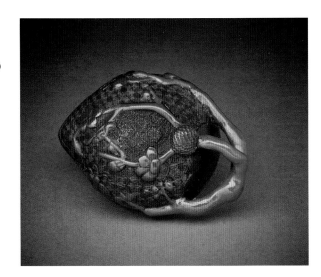

Herman Herzog,
American, born Germany
(1832–1932)

Forest with Heron
c. 1899
Oil on canvas
39 x 32 in.
(99.1 x 81.3 cm)
Gift of friends of the Harn
Museum
2013.28.1
Photo: Randy Batista
Poem: page 44

China

Leaf-Shaped Dish
Qing dynasty (1644–
1911), eighteenth century
Porcelain, wood
3 ⅜ x 3 ⅜ in.
(8.5 x 8.5 cm)
Museum purchase, funds
provided by friends of
the Harn Museum and
the Kathleen M. Axline
Acquisition Endowment
2008.24.2
Photo: Randy Batista
Poem: page 44

Nozaki Sadao, Japanese,
active early twentieth
century

Cricket Cage (Mushikago)
1930
Hanging scroll; mineral
pigments, gofun (clam
shell gesso), and sumi ink
on silk
9 ft. 2 ½ in. × 53 ¼ in.
(280.7 × 135.3 cm)
Museum purchase, funds
provided by the Kathleen
M. Axline Acquisition
Endowment
2017.14
Photo: Randy Batista
Poem: page 45

Author's Notes

pp. 1, 2–3: "A Scholar's Rock Looks at a Poet" and "The Monet Returns from Its Travels" were commissioned for *Samuel P. Harn Museum of Art at Twenty Years*.

pp. 4–5, 6–7: "Still Life with Dead Letter: Mme. Sévigné in New York" and "Vermeer in Japan" accompanied "Much Ado About Portraits," 2013.

pp. 8–15: "Postcards from the Tokaido Road" were commissioned for "Life is a Highway: Prints of Japan's Tokaido Road" and printed as a set of postcards by the Harn Museum.

pp. 16–17: "To an Inkstone" and "Two Glazed Bowls" accompanied a new installation of the Korean gallery, 2014.

pp. 18–22: "The Dead" and "Fold upon Fold" accompanied "Into the Fold: Contemporary Japanese Ceramics from the Horvitz Collection," 2014–2016. "Fold upon Fold" was printed in limited edition as a broadside by Ellen Knudson for the opening.

p. 23: "Skin of Clay": Akiyama Yō gave a demonstration of his sculpture techniques while he was visiting. He stumped the head of ceramics at UF, who thought she had figured out how he had built the huge piece on display.

pp. 24–25: "Ink Garden": The Cofrin Asian Wing has two gardens, the wet and the dry. The dry was an ingenious afterthought by the garden designer. The volunteer who tends it took a morning to show my poetry interns and myself the poetry and practice of a Zen dry garden. We raked! I became curious about the geology of the "toothed" gravel we raked, Florida being short of rocks. So I took a tiny handful to a geologist, who told me its tale.

pp. 26–28: "The Alley Behind Memory" accompanied the reinstallation of contemporary Japanese ceramics.

p. 29: "The Elephant God Speaks" was commissioned for the gallery guide to "Show Me the Mini," 2017–2018

pp. 26–35: "Small Monument in Memory of Winter," "Against Moonlight," and "Never Closer" accompanied the reinstallation of contemporary Japanese ceramics.

pp. 36–43, 45: accompanied "Show Me the Mini," 2017–2018.

DEBORA GREGER, Professor Emerita at the University of Florida, has been Poet-in-Residence at the Harn since 2012. She has published ten books of poetry.

Acknowledgments

Some of these poems appeared in the limited-edition anthology *Ink Garden* (Harn Museum of Art, 2015).

"The Monet Returns from Its Travels," "A Scholar's Rock Looks at a Poet,"(Debora Greger, *In Darwin's Room,* Penguin, 2017)
and in *Samuel P. Harn Museum of Art at Twenty Years*, (University Press of Florida, 2010)

"Postcards from the Tokaido Road," (*Birmingham Poetry Review,* 2016)

"Skin of Clay," (*Yale Review,* 2016)

Thanks to Jason Steuber and Allysa Peyton, Cofrin Asian Wing for this book and much else. The poems would not have been written had I not been taken under their wing.

Thanks also to the UF student interns who have joined me as poets-in-residence over the years. And to the Museum Night visitors who took part in the writing activities sponsored by us.